Cargo ships

Althea and Edward Parker

Illustrations by Peter Kent

Contents

A & C Black · London

Carrying cargoes

Bicycles and bananas, coal and cars, timber and toys, lathes and lightbulbs, oil and oranges, sand and shoes. Thousands of tonnes of all kinds of goods or cargoes are floating around the world in cargo ships. The sea is the main way of moving goods from one country to another. Ships have always been so important to trade that we often talk of 'shipping' something even if it is going by road, rail or air.

Before roads and railways, boats and ships were the only way of moving heavy cargo around. River barges and coastal ships carried things like grain, coal, timber and wool from town to town.

A general purpose cargo ship

An oil field support ship

We'd better get out of the way—fast!

Container ship

A naval support ship

A 123

A 'roll-on, roll-off' or 'ro-ro' ferry

A liquid gas tanker ship

Nowadays, many different types of cargo ship carry goods all round the world. Some are specialized, such as container vessels or refrigerator ships. Others carry general cargo in their holds and some, called VLCCs (Very Large Cargo Carriers) carry bulk materials such as cement, grain and iron ore. A special type of VLCC called a tanker carries crude oil from oil wells to refineries in Europe and America.

Floating supermarkets called naval supply vessels keep warships at sea supplied with food, spare parts and fuel.

Ferry ships, called ro-ro (roll-on, roll-off) ferries carry the big international container trucks on part of their journeys across continents.

Why ships float

Have you ever wondered how a big ship, made of steel and weighing tens of thousands of tonnes, can float? It floats for the same reason that a log of wood floats because both the ship and the log are lighter than the weight of water they push aside or 'displace'.

Anything floating displaces a volume of water. This creates an upwards force which is equal to the weight of the volume of water displaced. A big ship is heavy but the water it displaces weighs even more than it does and the upward force keeps it floating on the surface. The steel ship and the log are lighter than the water they displace because they contain a lot of air, which is very much lighter than water.

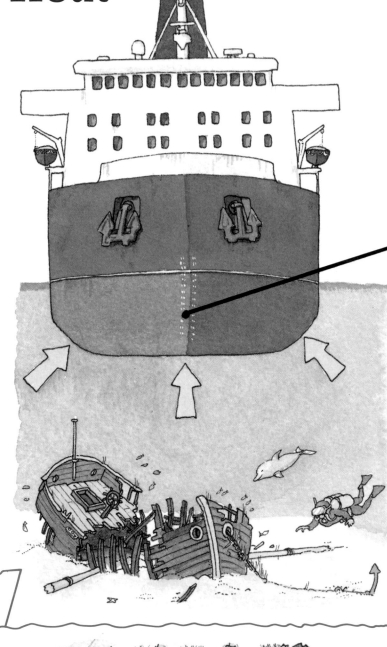

RICE-BREAKER

A wooden merchant ship carrying a cargo of rice sunk because the crew did not realize it was leaking. The rice soaked up the water and swelled so much that it broke the ship apart.

The volume of the ship underwater displaces the same volume of water.

The weight of the displaced water is more than the weight of the ship.

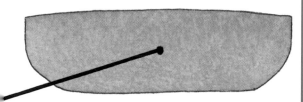

The displaced water 'tries' to get back into the space taken up by the ship. This creates an upward pushing force which keeps the ship afloat.

If you push down on a bath toy, you can feel the water pushing it back up.

I wonder what will happen if I stop pushing?

First boats

The first boat of any sort was probably just a log floating in a river, which people sat on and rowed along using branches as oars. This may have been a bit faster than walking but balancing on a log would not have been easy. The early boatmen would probably have spent more time falling in the water than sitting on their logs.

Here we go again . . .

The log boat was also not much use for carrying cargo. Something more stable with space for carrying things was needed. The raft was the answer to this problem.

5

People made raft boats out of practically anything they had, or could make, which would float. Logs tied together were common in places where there were plenty of trees. Rafts were also made out of bags of gourds (the dried seed pods of some plants), clay pots, animal skins blown up like balloons, bamboo poles or bundles of reeds. These rafts had a platform on top for the passengers and cargo.

Rafts, which were mostly used on rivers, were driven by oars or pulled by men or animals or allowed to drift with the current and steered by a large oar at the back.

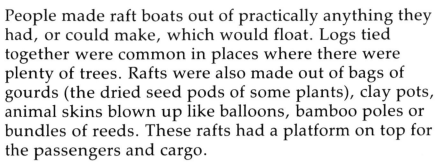

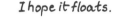
I hope it floats.

Raft made from tree trunks lashed together with ropes.

People also used sails to drive rafts. There is evidence of sails being used on Nile river rafts in Egypt as early as 5000BC. These first sails were large square sheets made of animal skins or woven matting fixed to a simple mast. This design had one big drawback. The sails could only drive the boat along in the direction of the wind and so, for many centuries, oars remained the main method of driving ships, even for big ocean-going cargo ships.

Steering oar

Raft made from animal skins blown up like balloons.

Cargo of pots of oil and jars of wine.

LEAFY SAILS

In the days before sails, a leafy tree may have been used as a primitive sail.

Kayaks and dug-outs

Rafts were good for river travel and short coastal voyages in calm weather, but they had several disadvantages when people wanted to go on longer sea voyages. The main problem was that rafts floated so low in the water that, in rough weather, waves continually broke over them. This would have been wet and uncomfortable for the crew and not very good for the cargo either. A raft is also slow, difficult to steer and hard work to row.

The development of the boat with a hollow body or 'hull' overcame a lot of these problems. Two methods of constructing hollow hulls developed more or less at the same time. These were the frame boat and the dug-out.

Dug-out boats were made by hollowing out the centre of a big log. Polynesian people were exploring far out into the Pacific Ocean thousands of years ago in boats like this.

The logs were sometimes hollowed out with small fires.

Inuit paddling a kayak in north western Greenland.

Frame boats were usually made out of lightweight timber tied together and covered with a waterproof skin of animal hides. The hides were sewn together. Boats were also made of woven rushes or reeds. These were often covered with pitch from natural tar pools to make them watertight.

People all over the world built frame boats and they are still being made today. The Inuit people of Northern Canada use frame boats called kayaks for hunting seals. These boats are very similar to the ones their ancestors made thousands of years ago, although they now use canvas for the covering instead of animal skins.

Frame covered with animal skins.

Timber frames are tied together.

I wish I had a sharper needle.

Animal hides are sewn together to make one big skin.

Wooden hulls

Boats with wooden hulls, made up from planks of wood fixed together, developed from a combination of the technologies of frame construction and the dug-out canoe. Side frames, hull planking and decks were added to the dug-out canoe. This made the boats more seaworthy, bigger, stronger and able to carry more cargo.

Over the years, as construction methods developed, the original dug-out part of the boat gradually disappeared. The boat builders realized that it was not necessary to dig out the log. Instead they built the hull by fixing wooden ribs and planks to a strong piece of wood on the bottom of the boat. This 'backbone' is called the keel of a boat. The front end or 'bow' of the boat is sharp to cut through the waves. The back end or 'stern' is much blunter.

The figurehead was usually a fierce animal or 'dragon'.

I'm on pillage duty today.

The hull was made out of overlapping planking fixed to the frame timbers.

10

Land ahoy!

The Viking sailor Eric the Red probably discovered America in a 'longship' like this one. He got his name from his bright red beard.

Very large ships driven by oars were built. Oar power was the main way of driving ships right up to the Middle Ages. Most big ocean-going ships carried sails just to help the rowers if the wind was going in the right direction.

Let's call it Vinland.

I think America might be a better name.

A Greek warship called a trireme. 200 oarsmen in banks of three could drive this ship at more than 15 kilometres an hour.

Sail power

Oar power was fine for warships carrying men into battle, but in cargo ships the large crew of rowers took up a lot of room and reduced the amount of space left for cargo.

Late in the Middle Ages, sails were developed which allowed the ships to sail in more or less any direction. Now bigger ocean-going cargo ships could be built which relied only on sails to drive them.

The new design of sails came about because people developed a better understanding of the way in which air flows over the surface of a sail.

An Arab dhow carrying a triangular 'lateen' sail.

Medieval cog

A Chinese junk with sails made from pieces of matting sewn together.

Oar-driven galley

Unlike the old sails, the new sails could be turned lengthwise in the ship instead of just going from side to side. This sail pattern is called fore and aft rig – the word rig being the name for all the sails, the masts and the ropes which control and support them. It works because the wind blowing past a sail creates a different pressure on each side. The pressure on the side of the sail that bulges is lower than on the other side and this pressure difference creates a sideways force. The sail is sucked along in the direction of the bulge.

The direction in which the ship actually goes is a combination of this sideways force and the way the water pushes on the hull. These two forces combine to make a forward driving force which is at an angle to the wind blowing on the ship.

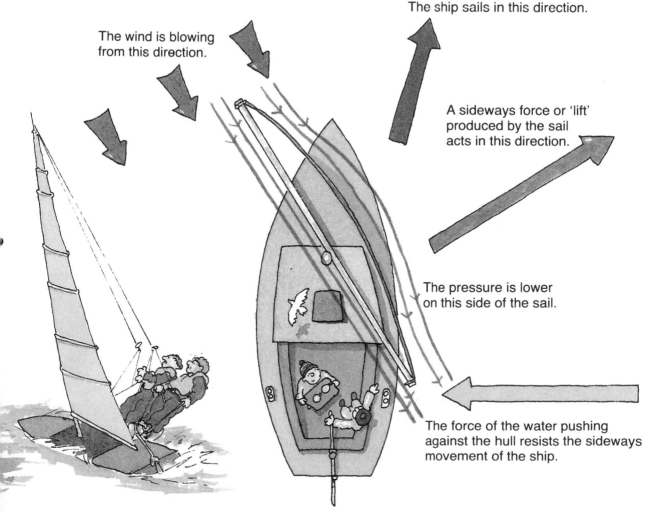

The ship sails in this direction.

The wind is blowing from this direction.

A sideways force or 'lift' produced by the sail acts in this direction.

The pressure is lower on this side of the sail.

The force of the water pushing against the hull resists the sideways movement of the ship.

Steering

The 'set' or angle of the sails to the wind works with the position of the rudder to make the ship go in a particular direction. Ships can sail in any direction except directly into the wind. If the direction or 'course' wanted is into the wind, the ship can 'tack' or sail sideways across the wind in a series of big zigzags. In a very strong wind, a ship may take many kilometres on each tack but only moves forward a short distance.

Sailors made use of winds called 'trade winds' which blew constantly east or west. The routes followed by ships using these winds became known as trade routes.

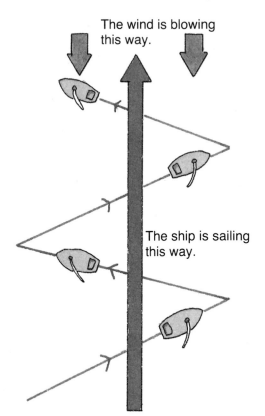

The wind is blowing this way.

The ship is sailing this way.

This ship is tacking in order to sail into the wind. The angle of the sails shows that it is sailing in almost the opposite direction to the wind.

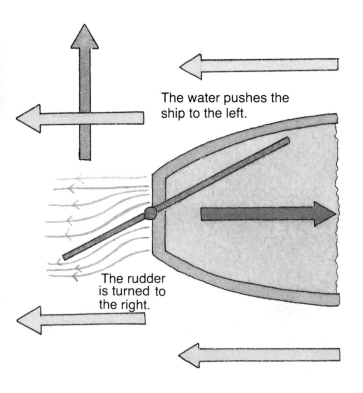

The water pushes the ship to the left.

The rudder is turned to the right.

The pressure of the water flowing past the rudder forces the stern of the ship in the opposite direction to the 'set' of the rudder.

The rigging on a big sailing ship was complicated, with hundreds of ropes controlling several hundred square metres of canvas. With ships driven only by sails, steering became more important. Steering an oar-driven ship was simple. The rowers on one side simply pulled harder than the rowers on the other side. Oar ships were easy to turn so they were used as warships for a long time.

A sailing ship however, needs a big rudder for steering. This developed from the steering oar into a solid timber slab hinged like a door. It was hung on the stern of the ship and controlled with a long pole called a tiller. In later ships, the rudder was connected by chains to a wheel which made steering easier.

A typical cargo list for this ship.

Madeira wine in casks ...... 500 gallons
Homespun cloth .... 200 bales
Nutmeg .... 1 cwt
Ivory .... 5 tons
Coffee beans .... 20 tons
White lead .... 50 barrels
Hempen rope .... 600 fathoms
Fine French brandy .... 30 casks
Silver bars .... Half a stone
Mahogany logs .... 100 chords

Mizzen mast

The masts carried poles or 'yards' which the sails were hung from.

Main mast

Foremast

The ropes in the rigging had different names according to the jobs they had to do. 'Halyards' pulled the sails up and down, 'sheets' controlled the angle of the sails to the wind and 'stays' supported the masts and yards.

Captain's cabin

Many merchant ships were armed with cannons to protect themselves from pirates.

Foresail

Cargo holds

Hull made of heavy wooden planks nailed or bolted to wooden frames. The gaps between the planks were filled or 'caulked' with hemp to keep the ship watertight.

The anchor dug into the sea bed to hold the ship in position. It was pulled up and down by sailors pushing a wheel called a capstan round and round.

Navigation

I told you I knew where we were.

The problem on an ocean voyage was finding out where you were. In the early days of shipping, when voyages were mostly coastal trips, sailors could find their position from landmarks such as familiar headlands, mountain tops and even particular trees. Out of sight of land however, a way was needed of working out the direction to steer and where you actually were. This is called navigation.

Early navigators observed the Sun and stars and used geometry to calculate the ship's position and the direction they needed to steer. We sometimes forget that our ancestors were every bit as clever as we are and that navigation was an advanced science by the time people were exploring the Pacific Ocean 2500 years ago.

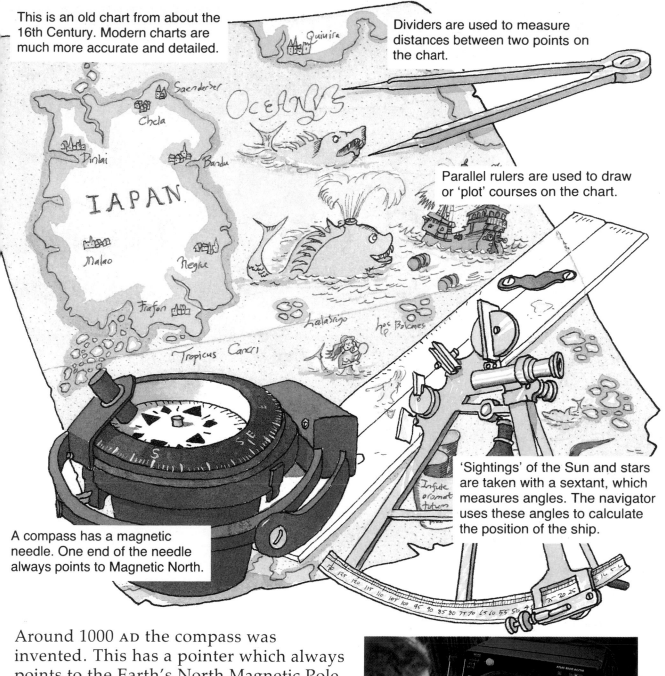

This is an old chart from about the 16th Century. Modern charts are much more accurate and detailed.

Dividers are used to measure distances between two points on the chart.

Parallel rulers are used to draw or 'plot' courses on the chart.

'Sightings' of the Sun and stars are taken with a sextant, which measures angles. The navigator uses these angles to calculate the position of the ship.

A compass has a magnetic needle. One end of the needle always points to Magnetic North.

Around 1000 AD the compass was invented. This has a pointer which always points to the Earth's North Magnetic Pole. Compasses made navigation a lot easier since sailors now knew exactly the direction they were going in even if they couldn't see the Sun or the stars.

Methods of navigation using compasses, observing the Sun, Moon and stars and using charts and clocks did not change very much until electronic systems were fitted in modern ships.

In a modern ship, the radar system shows other ships and geographical features.

The end of sail

Wooden, sail-driven cargo ships lasted, with very little change of design, for 500 years from the Middle Ages until about the middle of the 19th Century. Afterwards, ships started to be built in iron, partly because the supply of wood was running out and partly because much bigger ships could be built in iron.

Iron ships did not leak as much as wooden ships. After about thirty years at sea, a wooden ship was so waterlogged and leaky that the crew spent most of its time pumping the water out. In the 1850s, Norwegian ship owners made good profits by buying scrapped wooden ships very cheaply and keeping them at sea by pumping the water out with windmill-driven pumps.

We need more speed, they're beating us.

At about the same time as iron was replacing wood, sail power was gradually being replaced by steam engines. Sailors were reluctant to trust steam power, and so for a long time ships were built with both sails and steam engines. Sailors were, in some ways, right to be suspicious of steam. The early engines were big, inefficient and liable to break down. Engines rapidly improved though, and by about 1900 no more sailing cargo ships were being built.

Iron ships were built in a similar way to wooden ships. They had a keel at the bottom and a framework of iron girders with iron plates riveted to them.

The last and most beautiful of the sailing cargo ships were the American clippers, which carried tea from China and wool from Australia at the end of the 19th Century. Many were built in iron and some were converted so they could be driven by steam engines.

FIERY SHIPS

In 1883, the *Sirius* became the first ship to cross the Atlantic under steam power alone. The ship ran out of coal and the crew had to burn the furniture, deck planking and most of the wooden fittings to finish the voyage.

Modern cargo ships

The hull of a modern cargo ship is made from very big steel plates welded into a box shape. Steel girders along the length of the ship and frames from side to side give the hull the stiffness and strength needed to carry the weight of the engines and cargo.

The ship is divided up into different levels by floors called decks. The main hull contains the spaces where the cargo is stored. Depending on the type of ship, these holds may be great barn-like spaces or specialized storage containers such as tanks.

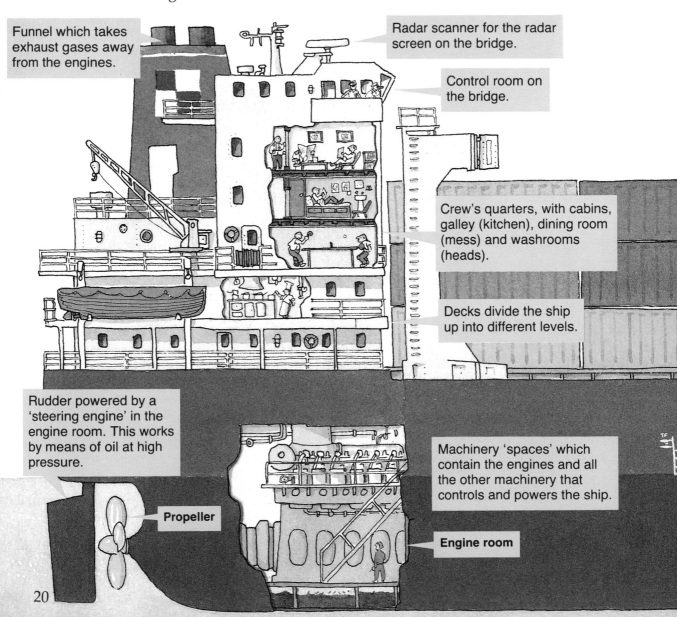

Funnel which takes exhaust gases away from the engines.

Radar scanner for the radar screen on the bridge.

Control room on the bridge.

Crew's quarters, with cabins, galley (kitchen), dining room (mess) and washrooms (heads).

Decks divide the ship up into different levels.

Rudder powered by a 'steering engine' in the engine room. This works by means of oil at high pressure.

Machinery 'spaces' which contain the engines and all the other machinery that controls and powers the ship.

Propeller

Engine room

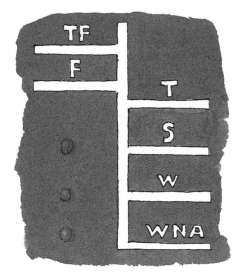

This line on the side of the ship is called the Plimsoll line after the man who introduced it. It shows how heavily loaded the ship is and if it is at the right depth in the water. The letters stand for different kinds of water. TF for instance, means Tropical Fresh water.

Three-quarters of the hull of a fully loaded cargo ship is under the water. The depth of water it needs to float is called its draught and a big ship can 'draw' 20 metres or more. This is why a big ship needs very deep water harbours and has to keep to deep water channels. In some places in the English Channel for instance, a fully loaded tanker has very little water under the keel.

A container ship with its cargo protected safely inside large metal boxes.

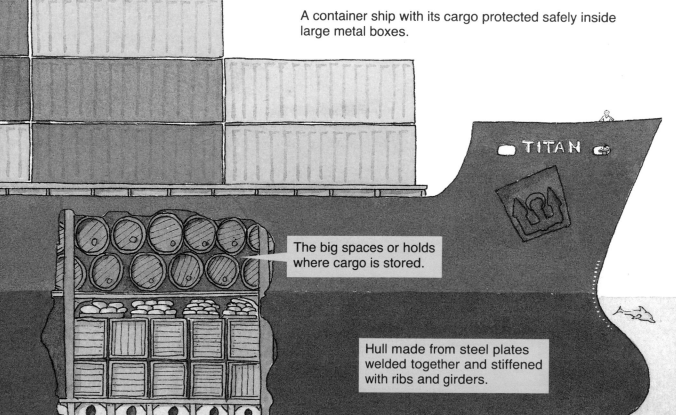

The big spaces or holds where cargo is stored.

Hull made from steel plates welded together and stiffened with ribs and girders.

Engines

A VLCC might weigh more than one hundred thousand tonnes when it is full of cargo and so needs very powerful engines. Its engines may develop 25,000 kilowatts of power, which can drive the ship at 27 kilometres per hour. This amount of power would be enough to light half a million lightbulbs or make about 100,000 pots of tea.

Nowadays, new cargo ships are fitted mainly with diesel or gas turbine engines. These have replaced the earlier steam engines, which were more expensive to run. Diesel engines in ships are very similar to the powerful, high-speed engines used in railway locomotives. These are big versions of the engines in buses, trucks and cars.

The diesel engine makes use of the fact that air gets hot when it is squeezed or 'compressed'. The engine has several cylinders, each with a piston inside. The pistons are connected to a crankshaft. As the pistons move up and down, the crankshaft turns round and round. This, in turn, makes the propeller shaft and the propeller turn round, which pushes the ship through the water.

1 The piston sucks air into the cylinder through the open 'inlet' valve. This is the inlet stroke.

2 Both valves are closed and the piston squeezes air into the top of the cylinder, making it hot. This is the compression stroke.

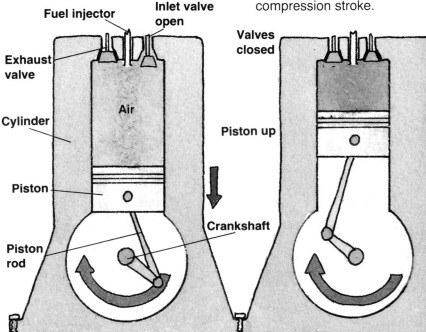

Fuel injector
Inlet valve open
Exhaust valve
Cylinder
Air
Piston
Piston rod
Crankshaft

Valves closed
Piston up
Crankshaft

The gas turbines fitted to some ships are very similar to the engines on jet aircraft. They work in a similar way to a windmill. The turbines are like the sails of a windmill and they are driven round by a 'wind' of hot gases made by burning kerosene fuel. The turbine turns a shaft which drives a gearbox. The propeller shaft and propeller are turned by wheels with teeth (gear wheels) inside the gear box.

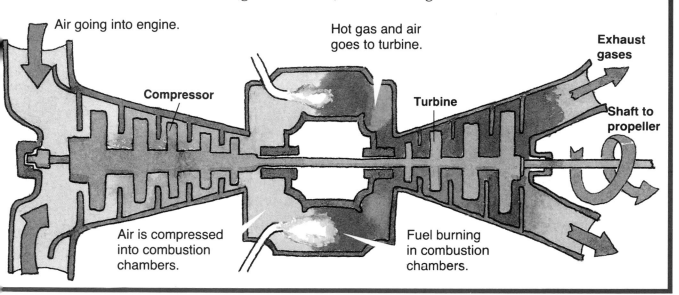

Air going into engine.

Hot gas and air goes to turbine.

Exhaust gases

Compressor

Turbine

Shaft to propeller

Air is compressed into combustion chambers.

Fuel burning in combustion chambers.

3 The piston is now at the top of the cylinder and fuel is being injected into the hot compressed air.

Fuel in

4 The heat makes the fuel explode and the expanding gases from the explosion push the piston back down the cylinder. This is the power stroke.

Fuel explodes

Piston down

5 The piston pushes the burnt and used-up gases out through the open 'exhaust' valve ready for the next inlet stroke. This is the exhaust stroke.

Exhaust valve. open

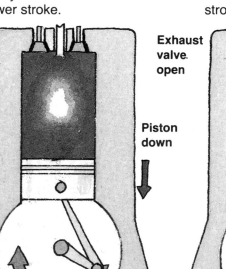

Some ships are powered by a combination of diesel or gas turbine engines and electric motors. In these 'power plants', the engines drive generators which make electricity. Motors convert the electricity into the movement of the propeller shaft. These engines are called diesel-electric or turbo-electric. They are very efficient because the speed of the propellers is controlled by changing the amount of electricity supplied to the motors. This means the engine can be run at its most economical speed.

The engine room is full of machinery. Electric generators produce power for lighting, heating and communication systems.

A diesel engine for a VLCC.

SHIPS WITH WHEELS

The Romans invented a paddle-driven ship in which men turned a handle to drive the paddles.

Put your backs into it lads, or you'll go back to rowing.

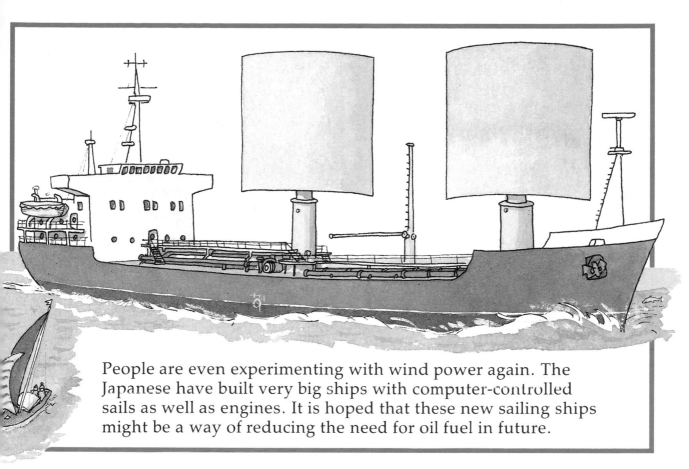

People are even experimenting with wind power again. The Japanese have built very big ships with computer-controlled sails as well as engines. It is hoped that these new sailing ships might be a way of reducing the need for oil fuel in future.

Ships may have one, two or four propellers. Very big ships usually have one big, slowly turning propeller. This is the most efficient way of driving them.

A propeller pulls water from in front and pushes it out behind, driving the ship along. It's like a screw driving through a piece of wood. Ships' propellers are often called screws because of this.

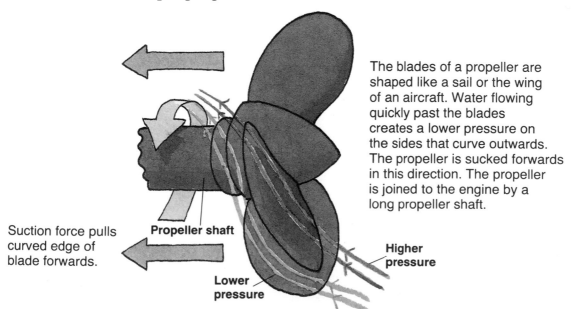

The blades of a propeller are shaped like a sail or the wing of an aircraft. Water flowing quickly past the blades creates a lower pressure on the sides that curve outwards. The propeller is sucked forwards in this direction. The propeller is joined to the engine by a long propeller shaft.

Suction force pulls curved edge of blade forwards.

Propeller shaft

Higher pressure

Lower pressure

Handling the cargo

There are several kinds of cargo ship. The VLCC which handles bulk cargo may be designed to carry 'dry' cargo such as iron ore or liquid cargoes such as oil or chemicals. VLCCs are the biggest kind of cargo ship. Smaller cargo ships may carry general cargo packed in sacks or crates or bulk cargo such as grain. Smaller tankers often carry refined oil products from a refinery to the loading depot. Container ships are designed to carry cargo packed in containers which can be loaded on and off road trucks.

Each kind of ship has deck gear for handling its particular cargo. A general cargo ship has cranes for lifting cargo aboard and hoists for lifting crates and containers in and out of the holds. Fork-lift trucks like the ones used in warehouses move packages around in the holds. Container ships are usually loaded by huge travelling cranes on the dockside.

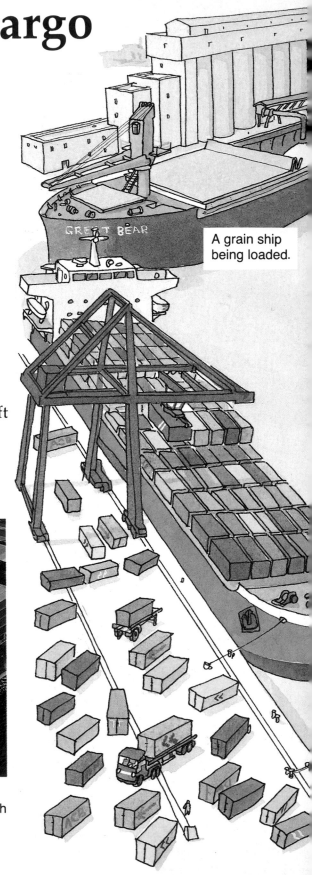

A grain ship being loaded.

A container ship is loaded by cranes which are controlled by computer. They record the position of each container on the ship so they can be unloaded in the right order.

Tankers have pumps for handling the liquid cargo. VLCCs even have bicycles on board to save the crew having to make the 1000 metre walk to the bow and back when they need to inspect the ship or work on the deck.

Sea-water often leaks into a ship and water has to be pumped out of the bottom part of the ship, which is called the bilges. Sometimes the water is pumped into the bilges deliberately to weigh the ship down so that it floats at the right height in the water. This is called ballasting and a VLCC sailing empty of cargo may pump in thousands of tonnes of water ballast.

This tanker is alongside a jetty unloading its cargo of oil into huge storage tanks.

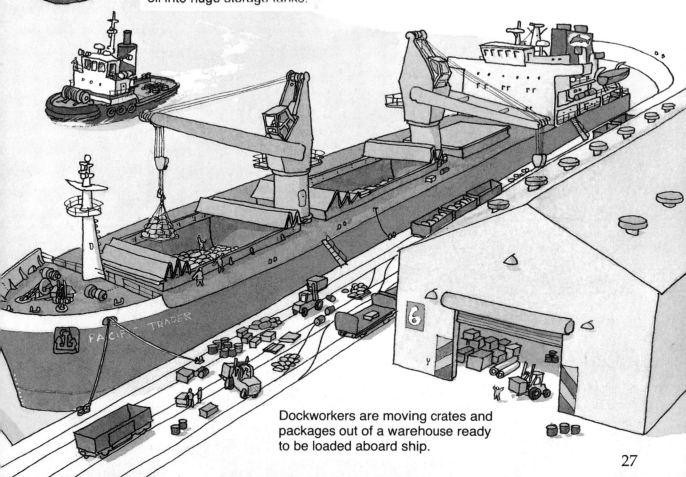

Dockworkers are moving crates and packages out of a warehouse ready to be loaded aboard ship.

Controlling a big ship

Radar display screen

Compass

Steering position

Engine controls and instruments

The bridge of a big cargo ship. The crew have a good view through the windows.

Modern ships are steered and controlled almost entirely from the bridge. Even a 100,000 tonne ship can be run by a crew of 20 with only five or six people on duty at any one time. The steering is controlled by hydraulic motors, which are worked by oil at high pressure. These motors transfer the movement of the wheel to the rudder through pipes. The power steering means that the wheel on a modern ship can be small, like a car steering wheel.

Ships' officers have instruments on the bridge to tell them if the ship is performing as it should. Navigation officers on modern ships can steer the ship using charts and compasses but now they also have complex electronic systems to help. Navigation equipment using signals from radio stations allows the navigator to 'fix' the ships' position anywhere in the world.

Although the bridge crew have to keep a look-out all the time, they have radar to warn of other ships in the area and to detect the position of coastlines, islands and icebergs. These show up in the dark and in fog while they are still many kilometres away. This gives the crew plenty of room and time to avoid the danger. A VLCC at full speed needs eight kilometres to stop, even with its engines full in reverse, and takes a circle of over 1.6 kilometres to turn around.

In the early days, steam ships were supposed to give way to sailing boats but nowadays skippers of small yachts would be very selfish to expect supertankers to stop for them.

Ships are in touch with their ports and bases by radio and you can even make an ordinary phone call to a ship through the ship-to-shore radio network.

WALKING THE PLANK

The word 'bridge' probably comes from the plank on Medieval warships that was used as a bridge to board an enemy ship alongside.

Safety and environment

The crews of modern ships have much better working
conditions than sailors in earlier centuries. Modern ships
have well stocked freezers and comfortable cabins. But
the sea can still be dangerous and many precautions are
taken to avoid accidents.

Modern ships carry very detailed charts showing the
position of dangers such as wrecks and shallow water.
An international system of buoys and lighthouses warns
the crew of dangers in their area. All ships have to obey
a 'highway code' of the sea which is designed to prevent
collisions. Many countries operate marine rescue services
using lifeboats and helicopters.

This man is cleaning up oil which escaped from a tanker and drifted on to a beach in Madeira.

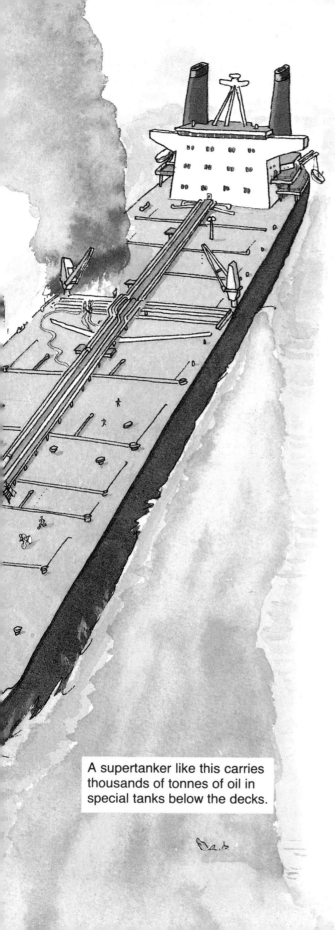

A supertanker like this carries thousands of tonnes of oil in special tanks below the decks.

Ships are occasionally lost in storms and accidents. The sea disasters that make the headlines almost always involve oil tankers. A big tanker carries millions of litres of sticky black crude oil which can make a terrible mess if it spills into the sea. Beaches often get fouled and wildlife suffers badly, particularly birds. But the oil spilt from a damaged tanker actually causes less harm to the environment than it would if it was burnt to fuel power stations and cars.

As long as teddy bears need to get from Hong Kong to Barcelona and radiator valves from Copenhagen to Sydney, ships will always be one of our most useful tools.

31

Index

First published 1992
A & C Black (Publishers) Limited, 35 Bedford Row, London WC1R 4JH

ISBN 0-7136-3534-7

A CIP catalogue record for this book is available from the British Library.

Acknowledgements
Edited by Barbara Taylor
Photographs by: Bryan and Cherry Alexander Photography page 9; ''K'' Line, Canada Maritime and CMB page 17, page 21; NEI Allen Limited page 24; P & O Containers page 26; Warren Spring Laboratory page 31.

The authors would like to thank Chris Corcoran of Maritime Studies Ltd, Camarthen for his invaluable help and advice.

Photoset by Rowland Phototypesetting Ltd Bury St Edmunds, Suffolk
Printed and bound in Italy by L.E.G.O. Spa.